What Possessed Me

Other books by John Freeman

Poetry

Snow Corridors, Rivelin Press, Sheffield, 1975
A Landscape Out of Focus, Galloping Dog Press, Swansea, 1978
The Unseizable, Stone Lantern Press, Swansea, 1978
A Vase of Honesty, Great Works Editions, Bishop's Stortford, 1979
Going Home, Rivelin Press, Bradford, 1984
The Light is of Love, I Think: New and Selected Poems, Stride Publications, Exeter, 1997
Landscape With Portraits, Redbeck Press, Bradford, 1999
A Suite For Summer, Worple Press, Tonbridge, 2007
White Wings: New and Selected Prose Poems, Contraband Books, 2013
Strata Smith and the Anthropocene, The Knives Forks and Spoons Press, forthcoming

Criticism

The Less Received: Neglected Modern Poets, Stride Publications, Exeter, 2000

WHAT POSSESSED ME

JOHN FREEMAN

First published in 2016 by
Worple Press
Achill Sound, 2b Dry Hill Road
Tonbridge
Kent TN9 1LX.
www.worplepress.co.uk

Cover image by Cathy Freeman
Author image by Cathy Freeman

Printed by imprintdigital
Upton Pyne, Exeter
www.imprintdigital.com

Typeset and cover design by narrator typesetters and designers
www.narrator.me.uk
info@narrator.me.uk
033 022 300 39

ISBN: 978-1-905208-36-4

Acknowledgements

Some of these poems or earlier versions of them have appeared in the following publications, and I am grateful to the editors concerned: *Agenda, Fire, Iota, Poems for a Liminal Age, London Grip, Poetry Review, Poetry Wales, Scintilla, Sentinel Literary Quarterly, Tears in the Fence, The Journal, The Lampeter Review, The Lonely Crowd, The Rialto, The Ware Poets Competition Anthology,* and *Wales Arts Review.* 'My Grandfather's Hat' won third prize in the National Poetry Competition, 2012.

Contents

I

Me and the Gatepost

On the front of the gate are three numerals
in hard plastic, the colour of clotted cream,
with screw-heads aureoled in rust. The post leans
as if exhausted, while its thickness tapers
to the shape of a pitched roof, bleached, pale grey.
On the slant surfaces ravines have opened,
a wave of wood, a wave of shadow. Something
about them speaks to me, independently,
I think, of the lavender, grey and blue,
growing to a sturdy hedge with gnarled stocks,
and the yellow privet by the other gate,
past which we push our bikes to the back yard.
Its fascination is unconnected
with my mother's vigorous red arm
and its pointed funny bone, the funnier
for the spread thickness of the muscled flesh
surrounding it, resting on top of the gate.
It has nothing to do, I'm sure, with her voice,
going on and on, talking not to me,
luckily, but to a passing neighbour,
even if the apparition is called up
by seeming to hear her say like one word
between you me and the gatepost as she leans
into some climax, some secret that isn't,
the flourish passionate, while all the time
the wavy fissures of that post and I,
in blissful silence, keep each other's counsel.

Interior With Red Linoleum

She is bending intently over the step
from lower to upper hall in our house.
A strong black rubber sleeve rounds out
its sharp edge. The lino beyond
is a pinkish red flecked with white
I've seen nowhere else. A threadbare
Turkey rug runs to the front door.
A nail under the lino is proud, she says.
I feel physically lifted up by the zest
her evenly spoken word gives the thing,
the haughty piece of ironmongery
refusing to accept its station in life,
raising its head above mere boards.
I admire her penetration of thought,
looking into the dark mind of a nail
and finding a way to say what she sees.
Then it breaks on me like first light
that this must be a traditional use,
a kind of speech not taught in school,
coming from generations unknown
of carpenters, wheelwrights, smiths.
She seems to embody them all by right.
I admire her reaching for *proud*
the way she handles a hammer, a saw,
a bit for a drill or a cobbler's last,
her attention all on the job in hand.
She is my mother, I am her son.
I think she is wearing a clean white apron
over a blue frock. The red lino glows.
I am as proud as a stuck-up nail in a plank.

Making a Meal of It

These days I'm lunch and dinner,
though I grew up dinner and tea,
not just a pretentiousness
of my own but a cultural shift.
As children we knew about lunch, of course;
some people had it, nobody did it.
But not even Mrs Wainwright
could believe her ears though, like us,
she must have heard clearly the first time,
when Mary Foster with her golden plaits,
white ankle socks, and a diction
in which every word was sliced off neatly,
asked when something was to be done,
so the teacher made her ask again,
and the class fell silent and the world stopped,
so that I see her to this day with her
doll-like prettiness, her self-assurance,
and hear her say even more distinctly,
before, pause, or after, pause, luncheon.

Poupard's Chiffchaff

Each time that haunting two-note phrase comes back
in Delius's On Hearing The First
Cuckoo In Spring, I think of Poupard, a boy
when I was a boy, taking his turn to give
a talk to the class about his hobby.
Aitcheson brought in a coil of rope,
eloquent in its thickness and its whiteness,
and spoke to us about mountaineering.
I can see him in front of the teacher's desk,
holding his rope impressively, clearly
the master of his subject, pausing
between something he had said and something
he was about to say. The only word
I can hear is Poupard's, with his soft voice,
gentle and thoughtful, well matched by his open
scholarly face, his noticeable ears,
his faint, self-mocking, unassuming smile,
repeating a word new to us, *chiffchaff*.
I seem to hear him say his own name, too,
but nothing else, just those two-note phrases
by turns, *chiff-chaff, Pou-pard, chiff-chaff*, and feel
an affection touched by wistfulness – I glimpsed
a world I would never enter, and a friend
I would never make who was at home there –
as enduring as it is mild and subtle,
seeing that smile, hearing that slow spondee.

Eliminating the Diphthong

His idea of a holiday was to go
by himself on a course in Normandy
about phonetics. At home he used to stand
in front of the bathroom mirror, watching
his mouth shaping the strange sounds we could hear
passing the open door, like the hoots of tugs
drifting up from the Thames on foggy days:
u-, u-, u-u-u; i-, i-, i-i-i,
all English diphthongs rigorously excised.
His vowels must have been pure enough
after all that effort, but he was fated
to lack the lightness like pattering rain
of a genuine francophone in full flight.
I shall always be able to see him stand
in the narrow space between the towels
on the rail and the discoloured bath, facing
the mirror with toothbrushes below it,
making short and long noises like signals,
I am turning to port, I have run aground,
I am reversing my engines. It was part
of the furniture like the chest of drawers
behind him, lined with asbestos, from which
we took face-flannels and cakes of green soap.
I think of it and catch whiffs of toothpaste,
Dettol, asbestos dust, and normality –
the taken-for-granted duration, *durée,*
of a life I could not always remember
to condemn as fleeting and inadequate,
or any other gloomy predicate
cast on it by adolescent wilfulness,
and which in spite of my vigilance therefore
entered me as eternal and infinite,
without need of justifying or explaining.

What Possessed Me

I cycled across London before dawn,
and as the sky paled heard a bird sing
such an echoing song I knew it must
be the nightingale Keats wrote about.
Up the terrifying dual carriageway,
with its lorries and exhaust from cars,
I kept on, one revolution of the wheel
after another, as morning became less
magic, more matter-of-fact. By afternoon
there were intervals without cars, views
over rolling green landscapes below.
I arrived at Stratford, bought a ticket,
and before the play spent shillings and pence
on a dainty meal that left me famished, angry.
I had meant to sleep in a bus-shelter,
but it was cold, and I cycled home
by moonlight, starlight, lamplight.
I found a lit blue and white machine
selling cartons of milk and as I drank
knew the pathways life was flowing
down in my arms and legs as surely
as if I could see them. At dawn
in a warm transport café my head
fell to the table-top. I was woken
with the breakfast I'd ordered,
passed out again between mouthfuls.

Round Hyde Park Corner a bus driver
gave me time and room. I never had
such courtesy from a road-user again.
I got home and looked in the mirror:
grime showing where wrinkles would be
half a lifetime later, a wild stare.
Why, said my mother, shocked.
It hadn't occurred to me to ask.
My father knew, and told us. I slept
for two days, ached for a week.

Friend of Truth

He hasn't been on speaking terms with the truth
for years, she'd say, pleased with her wit, and that
was as good a fair-weather sign as a fir cone.
Not that we used cones, nor seaweed. He would peer
at the hooded wall-thermometer in the yard
where sun never disturbed its accuracy,
call out the highs and lows the mercury
had pushed the thin black markers to, and pull them
back to the tops of the two silver columns
with the heavy horse-shoe magnet, red and grey,
its ends made concave to fit round the thin
glass of the tubes. Beside him bottled milk
would be pushing creamy ice cylinders
up through burst tinfoil caps, or trying not to
separate into blue and white by skulking
in water in a yellow plastic bucket.

He was on counting terms with truth all right,
seventy degrees Fahrenheit in the shade,
down to fifty-nine in the night, or sixty.
She scorned his promise to hoover the books
when he retired, and the implication she saw
in his sharing spoons to save washing up.
He must have said that once, and she preserved it,
adding, as if he ever *did* the washing up.
She was furious when he remembered
their courtship differently from her true text:
liar! You're not recording this, are you?

He made excursions into dead-pan humour,
pretending to read news from the paper
that started off believable: an increase
in accidents to trains passing our house
when the bedroom curtains were taken down.
That was the sort of offering that would call
her remark down from its case in the corner
like a fiddle or a concertina.
She'd play it as if she'd just invented it,
and we'd perform Being A Family.

My Grandfather's Hat

Most of the time I saw Granddad indoors,
first in his dark room with blue gas mantles
and a kitchen range and one tall window
in Poplar, then in the overheated lounge
of aunt Nell and Uncle George's new flat
in Morden when he was in his nineties.
But he came to stay in our house sometimes,
and it must have been when he was leaving
that I saw him wearing his trilby hat.
It was grey and sleek like a new plush toy.
No one had ever made our two front steps
more like a staircase in a stately home,
not even Mum with her polio feet.
Crowning himself slowly, his own archbishop,
holding on to a handrail like a sceptre,
he turned with no more haste than one of the ships
he had sailed in round Cape Horn as a boy
in another century, approached each step
like a descent to be addressed with ropes.
Grandly he lowered one foot, then the other,
while we watched him, silently exclaiming
vivat, and the black and white chess-board
of the path to the front gate stretched out,
like a long drive lined with waving flags.

Goodbye, House

Key words were in the baby's mother's tongue
set into English when we lived in Sheffield
and then in a village near Doncaster.
We'd search the *landau* for a lost *tototte.*
Rubbing her back through the snug Babygro
after holding her in the crook of an arm
while listening to her gulp, then gasp for breath,
watching the *biberon* slowly emptying,
we said, she needs to *rote* or she'll *dégueule.*
When she began to speak it was in Yorkshire.
The minders laughed over the way she said
fork, it was so like how they might have sworn
if they'd not been such a polite couple,
or offered to each other conjugal joy.
When we left the council house in Campsall
she was still no weight to carry and I held her
close to me going from one room to the next.
In each I waved to show her by example
and said, tata, *maison.* She understood,
because she held her own hand up and turned it
from side to side and said with such
tenderness and sadness, tata, *maison,**
it haunts me still and seems to summon for me,
with its melancholy and affection,
all the goodbyes we've had to say since then.

---

* *Note:* the italicised words mean respectively: pram, dummy, feeding bottle, burp, throw up, house.

Brought to Mind

Two or three times I was with Mum and Dad
on New Year's Eve and we crossed arms to sing
Auld Lang Syne and Dad gripped so tight it hurt.
He might as well have said in words, if I
press this hard can't your longer future flow
into mine? I'm terrified. Keep me alive.
If you can't, at least keep me in memory.
This may be the last year I shall see in.
I've often remembered how that felt to me,
but today I imagined how it felt to him,
all the value his life had built up destined
to blow away. I think he believed in
the absoluteness of being here more
than I ever did, and the finality
of ceasing to be. I don't know why I was
so afraid of it, he said to Jacqueline
in a dream, and to a medium I visited,
when I told her all this, I didn't *know*,
you see. She said he was still reading books.
It's not to reassure nor to placate
that I remember him every day,
invite him to go on living through me.
I do that anyway because I miss him.

The Bluebell Leaves

I used to lean out of the casement window
and look down at the dark glossy leaves
which came before the bluebells and remained
when the flowers were all gone over. The bells
were lovely while they bloomed, though not as big,
as plentiful, as crowded as I wanted.
Those fleshy dark-green leaves, shiny as if
sprayed with furniture polish, seemed to me
unnecessary wrapping, someone taking
too long to get to the point. Now I see them
under the leaning trunk of the apple tree
gleam in morning light on a day like this
when there's been a frost, and sun is dispersing
the mist above the playing fields beyond
the oak tree, railings, and the high embankment.
I hear a babbling sound of busy starlings.

At last I have crossed the country by train,
got here late last night to stay for a week.
Below, my mother bends over her tubs
and borders, wearing navy polyester
trousers and a neat blue cardigan,
a lilac blouse, her glasses on a chain.
Oh, and sandals. Her hair curls at the nape.
She bangs a saucepan with a mix of food
out on the sloping home-made bird table –
a slab of wood, untreated, tied with wire
coated in orange plastic to a tripod
which had been designed for storing saucepans,
though I don't remember it ever standing
next to the stove, a pyramid of steel.

Or do I? Forgotten things come back as if
for an instant they are present again.
The comical and dignified sight of her
bending low, seen from the window above,
is characteristically her, broad-beamed,
short, sturdy, her unsymmetrical legs
from polio camouflaged in those slacks.
That grey hair. The ringing sound made
by the thick saucepan against cracked wood.
Although in this memory I can't see them,
I know her eyes are the colour of bluebells.

Peasant Girl Hanging Clothes to Dry

In the Glyptotek, Copenhagen

There's been rain this morning but now
there's a pale sun brightening and even
some power in it. Going out into this
town garden, so familiar to her, she feels
exposed – it's not that mild – but safe,
steadied by the routine of her work,
almost unconscious in it. And yet
this sharp air and sunlight outside
steal up on her, like the neighbours' cat
stalking the sparrows, with a sense
of being twice as alive as normal
and, while she pegs the washing
methodically on the line, complete.
All the time this rawness, freshness,
and delicate warmth. Haven't you
lived such a moment and forgotten,
in childhood perhaps, in youth,
in earlier adulthood? What does this
painting by Berthe Morisot give you
so that you recognise it here among
great work by Monet, Cézanne,
Sisley, Pissarro, and Bonnard,
as the supreme poem in paint
of the collection? Give you back.

New Year's Eva

I don't know to this day how she did it,
but she got through the electric kettles
I bought her faster than other people
get through packets of biscuits or cigarettes.
It's not so long ago they hadn't learned
to switch themselves off after they had boiled,
though since I wasn't there to see them perish
I can't say that she didn't leave the lid up
and let the water steam away to nothing
while the coiled element hissed and burned out.
She was prodigal with water so maybe
she managed to splash the contacts so often
they went on terminal strike out of disgust.
I try to remember how many years
she still had left when I bought for myself
this sturdy travelling kettle I still use,
and have used now for more than twenty years.
I think of it and her wryly together.
'What are you going to do with that?' she asked,
when I first took it on a visit to her.
I was going to have time to myself
with a mug of tea before creaking downstairs
to make a pot of Sainsbury's Red Label
to take into her room and sit beside her
while we drank and she talked and I listened
with murmured ohs and ahs and nos and yeses.
It was part of the negotiation
I always had to have when I was with her,
as a condition of being able
to give and take with more or less good grace.
Last night having primed this good companion
and brought it up in case of waking early,
as I do, I rocked the switch to test it

and the red light wouldn't come on. I pushed
the lead into the socket, tried again,
kept trying, got a flicker and then nothing.
I thought it was a goner in the dying
minutes of December and her birthday.
Absurd, perhaps, to feel so much about it.
This morning, for some reason, it's all right.

In Apple Blossom Time

She used to tell me when the blossom
was coming out on the apple tree,
not so much because she cared for it
herself as because she thought
or hoped it might be an occasion
for me to make an extra visit.
But I was busy, we both knew that,
couldn't get away, and most years
I missed it until the spring after
the October when my niece Polly
found her lying on the kitchen floor.
I arrived late, slept in my old room,
and pulled back the thick curtain
suddenly next morning. The pain
was as acute as any I ever felt
when the dazzling pink and white
flowers of the unpruned tree
in full sun only inches from the north-
facing window hurt my eyes.

Botham's Ashes

For Irene Fawcett

We were going to go camping – not far,
and just for a night. Her world, not mine.
I was slow to be ready to leave, sitting
in that old wooden armchair with studs on,
watching Ian Botham hit fours like sixes.
I thought you didn't like him, she objected.
I shook my head. I'm changing my mind.
To make a point, when I was set to go, she
watched the repeat of a Wimbledon final,
which had also been a classic of its kind.
I remember a stuffy tent by a stream,
being a fish out of water, getting bitten,
and the distance between us, unbridgeable.
The day after, without hearing the news,
I was in work, handing marks to Irene.
We got to talking about Botham's heroics.
What an innings. Wasn't it glorious.
Even if, I summed up, in a lost cause.
Irene looked at me as if I was mad.
You do know what happened, don't you?
she asked. Australia had collapsed,
Bob Willis bowling as if in a trance.
England had won. I went down on my knees,
on the thin carpet tiles of her office,
and touched my head to the green nylon fuzz,
my arms stretched fully out in front of me.
I did it spontaneously, didn't think twice.
I've never done anything like it before
or since. But then, neither has England.

A Man I Used to Know

I met a man the day before yesterday
who used to know a man I used to know.
We praised him from our different points of view.
But what I think of now is just the way

we used to walk together by the river.
I think of him and hear him talking to me,
and see between the pillared trunks of trees,
the dark trunks of the lime trees, shining water.

The path we walked on, only half made up,
had humps and hollows, stones and puddles, mud.
To get there we had crossed a busy road.
Friends for a while, we talked and walked in step.

There was no falling out between us, just
something that needed our intense exchange
had run its course and we became like strangers.
Everything happened, I think, for the best.

No regrets. Just a sustaining memory
of shining water seen among dark limes,
two friends walking part of the same way home,
that like an unexpected gift comes back to me.

Message to a Priest

I got talking to an Irish priest in Rome
when we were waiting for the plane to London.
He had been living in Algeria
where people had been tortured on both sides,
but it was the comfortable West that brought
his only bitterness, when he spoke the word
progress with heart-aching sarcasm. I answered,
in everything except wisdom and kindness,
you mean, and something must have given me
the confidence and conviction to add,
to this man who had seen and lived so much
I hadn't, and could hardly even guess at,
still, there are good people everywhere. He looked
as if I'd given him a new idea,
or had been sent to tell him not to despair.
Take care of your health, he said urgently,
as I rolled a cigarette. We found each other
exotic, complementary in our difference,
and wanted to go on talking, and did, till
we were on the big Alitalia plane
and forced to separate. We stared goodbye
yearningly, briefly, pressed by passengers
wanting to move up the aisle we were blocking.
We ought to have exchanged addresses, written
to each other, become friends, met at least
once, if only years later, to celebrate
the mystery and gift of such encounters.
We both believe in the power of thought,
otherwise known as prayer, and I am sure
he has prayed for me and knows I think of him.

There is no reason he'd ever read this. If
you know a priest who worked in Algeria,
and may have flown from Rome to London in
1986 or thereabouts, tell him
I miss him, and the letters we never wrote,
and stopped smoking on Easter Day, two thousand.

It Was Us

Something led me to mention the time
twenty years earlier when we had stayed
in a cottage on the Isle of Wight,
our brief apogee, and she laughed
softly, sadly, deprecatingly.
I insisted, that was us, *c'était nous*.
She stopped laughing and accepted
the point I was making, whatever it was -
perhaps that our lives had been as real
as her having to let go of life was,
and that the understanding between us
now could connect with the harmony
then, the nearest we ever came.
I'd swum and talked, she'd danced and sung,
we'd walked by the sea and under trees.
Outside there had been cold rain and wind,
bracing. Inside was an open fire, stillness,
a vase of honesty and tall grass
on the mantelpiece that became
an emblem of that time, our time.
C'était nous. That settled, we got on,
me helping her as well as I could
with what she had to go through alone,
but able to accept my company
and loyalty right up to the tree-line
or the snow-line, and even beyond,
where the love welcoming her was
more than my own, I could feel it
borrowing my face to smile at her, see it
in the way she smiled at something through me.

The Exchange by the Stile

Let it be creation, let it be even
illusion, the sense of a coherence
in the story we tell ourselves of ourselves,
isn't it a story worth telling? We have
only the present moment, they say, breathing
in, breathing out, but what of how, driving
along the humming dual carriageway
in early May, I notice the beginnings
of small new leaves on trees where a stile guards
the path I used to walk along the river,
often alone, but one time with my father,
and feel a presence here as delicate
as the tender shoots not fully open.
Because I forget what either of us said
at this spot, I remember, driving on,
what he said later after we had skirted
the playing fields under the trees beside
this same river, the other side of it –
we'd have crossed it on the springy footbridge.
We were deep in placid communion,
about to leave the green part of the walk
to cross a busy road and head for home.
I touched his arm and we turned and stood still,
seeing the grass and the tall woods behind us,
and he said that looking back was something
he wished he'd thought to do and done more often.
He meant it literally about his years
of walking, cycling, and exploring, but then
the hidden meaning in it overtook him,
and we both heard it in the same instant,
ambushed, together, by unspoken feeling.

Whatever it was that happened and was said
at that stile I flash past on my journey,
or merely passed unsaid but felt between us,
it was present in that later retrospect,
the two moments fused into one moment,
infusing this one, not by an act of will,
but as fragrance taking me unawares,
like the penetrating scent of lilac
that caught me yesterday by the front gate
taking me back to mornings in my childhood.
We live in so much more than just the present.

My Father Swimming

Perhaps it doesn't need more understanding
than I've had of it all these years, seeing
in my mind's eye my father swimming
in a river where it passes between bluffs,
on two occasions, fused: once when I, fifteen,
would have gone with him if I hadn't been sick
on the coach, and walked back to the hostel,
and once before even my brother was born.
I think of that as their real honeymoon.
When he went the second time he was alone.

He swam in solitude and became again
the man he'd been, young, hopeful, and in love;
and so serene and settled he looked out
as a baby looks outward from being fed,
engrossed in some object across the room
as in the focus for a meditation.
Happiness freed him to swim in the river
as if dissolving in the world around him,
slipping out of limitation and into
the water that received him, and the landscape,
the famous gorges they had come to visit.

She didn't swim in those days, she learned later.
I see her sitting on a rock, watching.
He would have felt her eyes on him, moving
with the water and against the water.
He must have felt them again, going back,
looking up at the sky above the cliffs –
I imagine them steep, a rich red colour,
like some I've passed through in the same country –

seeing the river stretch out deep and broad.
I think he must have worn the boundaries
of separateness as lightly as he wore
a single piece of cloth, or even less,
swimming naked, or almost, in his heaven.

II

Swallows

Cool morning, scorching afternoon. A walk
through yellow fields, now across this farmyard.
On one side of the path in the air, a twitch,
a flicker, then another flicker, winking
in and out of gaping semi-darkness.
I step aside under a towering doorway.
Up there in the gloom, among the rafters,
a concentration of blackness is stirring
around a bubbling centre of dark life.
Back at the bright entrance there are four, five,
six chances to unriddle the sudden blur,
the curving wings, forked tail, flashes of white,
snipping sounds like a busy hairdresser's.
I blunder back out into the daylight
and re-join my companions where the path
opens on a deserted lane. Above us,
on telegraph wires in swags over a hedge,
a row of them seem queuing to be admired,
silhouetting on blue their slinky grace.
Then there are cream teas in a farm garden
while, at the periphery of vision,
shadows are swooping against walls, and beyond
living shapes transforming wires to staves,
whispering their music into the darkness
of memory like a nest high in a barn
they will return to, summer after summer,
into which, from the paths of careful thought,
I will step aside to be astonished
again as they explode out of nowhere,
past me, to the dazzling summer sunshine.

Wimpole Hall

For Steve Gibson

The folly's a good one, so the stone arch
of the pointed gothic window, lean and spare
above the massive gateway, in between
the only partially ruined tower at one end
of the front wall and the nearly not at all
ruined one at the other, looks authentic,
as well as picturesque against the blue
of this mid-March early afternoon sky,
and could be Rievaulx, Tintern, Bolton, Fountains.
It may be tosh, but it's intelligent tosh.
The walk up sloping turf from the little stream
is a challenging stretch after a fortnight
in which I haven't had time to walk enough
and, between the hours in the car yesterday
and the hours in the car later today, almost
a life-saver. There are free-standing trees,
and we linger under one of them to decide
what kind of oak it is, Turkey or Common.
Someone remarks on a low branch as big round
as the chests of the shire horses we've seen
pulling visitors on a painted wagon.
It stretches out to the length of ten men
laid end to end, parallel with the ground.
I think of famous cantilevered bridges.
The fissured bark is mossed and tinged with green.
I linger to take photographs, the last
a farewell shot, having turned downhill, framing
the whole harmonious shape, side to side
and top to bottom, so that nothing's cut off,
but the whole picture area is filled.

I catch up with Steve, who is nearest to me.
Will Wimpole Hall figure in a poem,
he asks. He has told me he never reads
poetry. He'll read this. I don't know, I say.

Sunset on the River

I didn't think about the light until you
told me this path along the river Lea
was where you used to run with your friend Jan.
It was one of your centres of the world.
My hand closed over the camera I'd slipped
into my jacket and forgotten about,
and I took photographs of you, smiling,
with the houseboats and the lock behind you.
Then the evening sunlight slanted almost
horizontally across the land and lit
the bare slim trees, with their slanting branches
lifted like skinny arms of eager children
tinged green and golden with the rising sap,
and now spectacularly more golden.
I took one more picture of that light, rising
it would be as true to say as falling
on the trees and your hair and smiling face,
seeing that it was transformative.
We walked on, keeping an eye on the time,
and the moment merged with the flow of moments,
until we saw the pictures properly,
days later, on the screen. I was surprised
how well that golden light had been recorded,
which at the time I didn't dare expect.
In fact it looked an even deeper colour,
and for a moment I thought it better
than being there had been, until I realised
that good as they are, and I'm glad I took them,
the pictures lack not only the fresh air,
the context of the walk, the sense of presence,
but the brightness of the living daylight,
which is both softer and more powerful.

A Walk at Mawgan Porth

We'd been together for most of the day
by the time we drove down a hill and saw
breakers speeding towards a yellow beach
in a narrow bay huddled round by cliffs.
Spray flew up where extravagant crests
knocked themselves into fragments on the rocks.
I'd remembered waves coming in aslant,
but not, I said to you, like this, thinking
maybe the weather had been quieter.
We carried my things into the old house
and the others arrived. Soon you drove on
to stay fifty miles further south with friends.
When I could I walked down the steep road, shrank
from four-by-fours racing round hairpin bends,
cut through a car-park and was among dunes,
marram grass, wet sand, winding rivulets,
half-buried shells. The waves looked about the same
as ten years earlier when I'd been here.
Seeing them from above had made them seem
even more to crowd on each other, sweeping
impatiently, diagonal to the shore.
With the road left behind I felt the wind
catching hold of me and I was surprised
at the same moment by an unhappiness
mixed up with something more ambiguous.
I sat in judgement on this sudden weakness,
accusing it of the worst things I could:
what I missed was just security, your
solid support, your happening to be
the person filling that role. As these charges
were read out you seemed to be standing there
in silent dignity rebutting them.

It was you whose absence was doing this.
I went down the beach to the water's edge,
taking off my hat before the wind could.
Everything yesterday was secondary
to that walk by the wildness of the sea.

To Southerndown And Back

Journeys shorten as they grow familiar.
What used to seem like an expedition
can now be almost lightly undertaken.
You're scarcely out of the other side of town,
with rolling views and low hills to the north,
when you see below you the turning off
the main road which is, actually, straight on –
it's the dual carriageway that veers inland.
You indicate, though you don't have to turn,
and soon you're recognising a village
and looking out for half-remembered choices,
left at a T junction, right at a fork.
Once you are on to that next road something
lifts inside you and expands, like the view
off to the west with the green river plain
and the ruined castle, a sense of breadth,
allowing the sky also to open out,
while ahead of you is that first hit, the rush
of seeing the living sea again at last –
you didn't know how much you've been missing it,
satisfyingly wild beyond the sands.
And as usual here, though not quite always,
there's plenty of clear sky between clouds, partly
because the air is usually moving,
though not always as fiercely as today,
as you'll realise when you finally get out.
First you follow the road as it curves round
eastwards under the hill with sheep, away
from the widening estuary below,
until there's a narrow road winding steeply
down to the first beach car park, which you ignore

because you're on your way to somewhere else,
enjoying the sea views and the blue above.
And here's your turning with a dead-end sign,
TRAETH, and it's vertical, and here's the bay.
Here are the extensive grey-walled gardens,
being restored though the mansion has gone,
and here's a space next to a dozen cars,
and there's no-one wanting money today
in exchange for a permit, and you stop,
decide what to leave behind, what to take,
and out you get and the air is freezing,
so much colder than it looks, and that wind
gives you a slap and a buffet, a foretaste
of how it will be at the top, on the cliffs,
when you begin to wonder how much stronger –
not a lot, you suppose – it would have to be
to lift you up and hurl you over the edge,
but it's OK, you're heavy enough to stand
and to stand it, and meanwhile out there
the west-end spotlight of sun through slate clouds
is marching its shafts of light over the stage
of the bay where silver-gilt waves dazzle you,
and the wavelike patterns in shiny black shale
on the foreshore are as satisfying
as they always are, and you're really here,
and it hasn't taken any time at all,
and you wonder why you don't come more often,
and the journey home by a different route
is still not so familiar as not to
be a discovery, with its changing views,
and the light is bright and sharp all the way.

Blackbird and Magpies

There was such a commotion overhead
among the branches that she looked up,
and there was a click-clicking blackbird,
attacking two clack-clacking magpies
three times its own size, darting at them.
A nest. So she shouted and hissed
and, seeing they had not just a blackbird
but an angry human being on their case,
the magpies flew off. Telling the story,
she gestures to show how the blackbird
flew down to the ground right in front
of where she stood, and she leans slightly
forward, as in an oriental greeting,
and we as good as see the magic bird
bowing to her on the grass before her,
then flying off at once on urgent business.
Oh we are all compromised, overlaid
by accidentals which obscure what we mean.
To me that was the song, the retelling
in which we relived with her the bird's blessing,
returned for her help to the bird, the music
of what she is distilled, disclosed, applauded.

Summer Solstice, Cornwall

The day seems endless. There's a welcome cooling.
The light has softened now but the long shadows
though not sharp, are deep, defining, frequent
in the close-packed field of tall green wheat,
light and shade alternating densely. Each stem
moves to a different rhythm in the breeze.
Along the lane white roses, pink-edged, silky,
are scattered thinly here, and thickly there,
among red campion and glossy oak leaves.
Gates closed or open leading into fields
show us the corn one side, brown sheep the other,
heads down, moving with the alertness
Trappists must acquire by keeping silent.
On the opposite hill across the valley
cows graze, ochre and white in dark and dazzle.
Where the road becomes all hedges, no more gaps,
we turn and stroll back, still sometimes glimpsing
the burning gold of the sun above a tree.
The day's crumpling-up of mind and body
from travel and from thinking about details
uncreases like a sail catching the breeze.
Stone houses with their flowering gardens,
each in its own space, make their quiet statements.
We hear the running water of the millrace.
Popular music from another era
drifts towards us from a cottage somewhere.
Gnats dance, ascending and descending angels.
The year is at its height, and takes us with it
to being fully open like wild roses,
wanting only this, nothing more than this.

Seagulls at Play

The clifftop path takes a big step sideways
above a rocky cove beset by gulls.
It's a breezy morning. We stand and watch
as the birds angle wings to rise and circle,
float on invisible currents up and down.
They seem to be doing it for the fun of it,
children running from swings to roundabouts,
but silently, without haste, gracefully,
like pensive adult skaters on a lake.
It becomes clear the summit of the cliff
must be the top of a steady flow of air
funnelled up and round by the rocky sides
until the wider space where we are standing
slackens the pressure as a loosened string
might let a bundle of sticks fall sideways.
I see one gull – I'm sure it's the same one –
spiral to the spot where I've been standing,
position itself, lift its tail towards me,
showing the neat soles of two webbed feet
as if to be inspected, and glide off,
disappear from sight, and in a minute
come back and do it all again, climbing
unseen steps to slide down after pausing
at the top to ready itself and savour
the anticipation, then letting go.
I savour it too, those lifted tail feathers,
the trim pink feet lined up like tiny shoes.
And off, and down, and circling up and back.
All the other gulls are banking, wheeling,
their long and elegantly tapered wings
creating silent rhythms on the sky
above the sparkling sea, turquoise and purple.

As I watch them at eye-level sailing
so nonchalantly, without visible means,
for a moment I think I could step forward,
holding my arms out wide, and be like them.

Sea Air

Not the most promising prelude to a walk –
the bright morning gone on family business,
packing up the holiday cottage, a drive
with home already in our thoughts, and now
a prosaic pay-and-display car park,
and the clouds gathering, rain on the way.
But here are the six of us winding up
a path away from clutter and vehicles,
towards the cliffs, past one of the finest
wild-flower meadows, purple, yellow, and white,
I've ever seen, and our loosening muscles
beginning to brace, when on the ear there comes
like the sweetness of welcome wood-smoke
where friends are gazing into flames, winding
into the sense with a similar fragrance,
a reel being played on a fiddle somewhere,
getting louder until we see, standing
on a patch of grass in front of a hut,
a woman playing to herself and us,
with no hat for money or any other
solicitation, just the beauty offered,
that sweet sound of the fiddle the tune shows off;
and it seems one with the fresh air we breathe,
the views of sky and fields and open sea.
We heave ourselves up and down the footpath
from cove to overlooked vertiginous cove,
forgetting everything except where we are,
until we come back down in the rain
and hear the forgotten violin playing
as sweetly as before and as much welcome,
as transformative, and when we pass

the woman is inside the hut, door open,
playing on to herself still, and making
a music of the land, the sea, the sky,
joining blood to spirit, forever to now,
a dancing air with such a silken tone.

Gardener's Friend

There's a robin in our garden again,
hopping close whenever we're out there working.
This one's different from the one last year
which increasingly seemed to be trying
to say something urgent as if time was short,
but kept his dignity like a dying prince.
This year's is more artlessly confiding,
like a child putting his hand into yours.
The feathers on his back are ruffled-looking.
He's not so young that he doesn't seem to ask
that aching question the other seemed to ask,
without being able to say what it is,
leaving you with the responsibility
of having a pain brought to you to heal,
just the confiding question and the ache.
All we can do, and we do it separately,
comparing notes afterwards, finding we've each
responded in the same way, is talk to him
as if he understood, reassuringly,
about what's happening and what we're doing.
He hopped up on a dead gooseberry bush
I was digging out and looked at me sideways.
Isn't it a strange thing, I said to him,
pausing from pushing the garden fork in
and levering the stem out by the roots,
to be alive and conscious, and not know why?
He'd helped me see that we had that in common.

What We Have in Late November

What we have in late November is the sky.
Having fallen asleep in full daylight
I woke to see all the ends of the Plough,
perfectly framed, filling the window space.
Last night I went outside just to look up
and saw Orion with his famous belt,
his trailing sword, its fecund nebula,
back in his winter station overhead,
surrounded by a scattering of frost
and Cassiopeia's landmark W.

This morning all the myths have fallen down.
Last night's stars are sparkling in the hedge
and any surface they can get a grip on,
metalwork and windscreen and wood bench.
The grass is like the Milky Way as seen
from Hubble or an observatory
on the least light-polluted mountaintop.

It's not all night and morning. Yesterday
after a sunny afternoon I saw
in the mirror the west turn turquoise,
then green, washed pure, luminous-numinous.

When the light was coming up today
bands of soft pink hung motionless on blue,
a Rothko without human agency.

November Christmas

The sun is out and the thaw has begun. I wear wellingtons for the first time this winter, but shoes would have done. In one direction three children are snowballing; we walk the other way.

> imprinting the verge
> I hear you call out – the road
> is sliding from you

Parts of the surface are dry, others covered in a thin layer of water that may be ice, or snow that may be icy. We reach the post box and, instead of following the road as it veers left, we turn right into the lane that gets narrower as it winds for about twenty yards so you can't see what's ahead. When we happen on Gordon standing opposite his house, it is as if he has popped up from nowhere. His long, craggy face is framed by a soft hat with earpieces. We greet him. I'm not fussed about it, he says. This will be all gone by lunchtime. I think how much of the spectacle I missed yesterday by not stopping to stare, but I was photocopying against the clock, and then talking to the class.

> smiles as I make jokes –
> students looking beyond me
> at thick, fast snow-flakes

If he is not fussed, what is Gordon doing here? I think he is like Grumpy, not wanting Snow White to see him smile. That was all covered an hour ago, he gestures, and I'm not sure if he means the shining black roof or the topiary trees shaped into almost perfect globes, like green and white toffee-apples. They were like ice creams, he says.

Look out for ice round the corner, he adds. I fell there in January, I answer, and was sore for days. We tell him we are going to walk round the village, down this lane and up the longer one, and back by the top road. Be careful, warns Gordon, the cars come tearing down there. We know. You've got to live dangerously sometimes, I call back over my shoulder, and you say, I'm glad I haven't got a Gordon's-eye-view of the world.

even the branches
of the brambles picked out
as if each was loved

Now the views open up – black trees against white fields. To our left, the south, a bush is hung with lights – drops of melt-water lit up by the low sun on the far side of them.

crunching over snow
I stop to feed my eyes –
a special silence

It's not that absence of noise is remarkable here; these lanes lead only to a few houses and farms. But now there is a tingling quality to the stillness.

we listen to the quiet –
an unseen horse nearby
whinnies its praise

There are plenty of horses round here but they move and are moved from field to field. We haven't seen any yet today. Are they in stables because of the snow, or some of them? From the farm on the hill a dog barks several times, and a horse, perhaps a different one, perhaps not, whinnies once. I wonder if whoever invented the octave was incited to it by hearing that descending scale.

what's all this whiteness?
asks the distant dog – a horse
reassures him

We reach the bottom of the hill and turn sharp right, and begin to plod up the slope. We stop to look through a gate.

a man in dark clothes
with his dog in the middle
of a white field

At the top of a hill where trees mark a tiny settlement we glimpse the rich chestnut colour of a single horse. We carry on up, listening for cars. We hear one and walk back to a passing place to wait. A couple of weeks ago the tractors were everywhere, trimming the hedges. They look very neat now, as if they'd had an army haircut. But the snow picks out everything and shows there are still curving twiggy branches all the way up the lane. I stop from time to time to admire the effect of the sparkling snow decorating them. On one branch the line of white, perhaps beginning to slip, looks as if it is spiralling round it.

November: Christmas
comes early – tinsel wound round
the hedgerow branches

Looking ahead up the road, still the curved branches springing out from the pollard trunks seem to echo each other, without ever being identical, every one distinct with its white coating. I press against a hedge to give a car room and look back. You have retreated to a passing place and are out of sight. The car speeds up – he can't see you either. You come up behind me calling, did you hear me swear at him?

We are close to the first turning, and instead of going on up the hill we take it. This short lane connecting the two parallel roads rarely sees a vehicle pass, and anything there is will be going slowly. There are fields on both sides, behind hedges allowing intermittent views.

this is where they were hiding –
ten chestnut ponies
by the white field's edge.

On the other side, unusually, there are sheep, a few, with very shaggy black coats. We stare at them but they blunder past, muzzles to the ground, uninterested in us. You put on your animal voice to speak for them, their disregard. Look, you say. A black and white sheep with war paint on its face, a mostly black body. As it retreats we see it has a white tail, so long and thick I mistake it at first for a leg.

dad was the white sheep
of our family – but I
try to keep it dark

I catch one of those unnerving brown eyes with straight edges to its yellow pupil.

We come back to the road which has more houses on, though not enough to be numbered: we pass Cartref, Ty Deryn Nos, Afallon, Restharrow, and back to our own home. We haven't seen a soul except Gordon, not counting the three cars we stood back from. Two boisterous children come towards us and a few yards behind them, head bent, face pale, mouth curved downwards, a smaller one, left out, left behind.

grownups suppose all
children have a happy time
just because there's snow

We can't do anything to help the poor mite and turn into our drive.

my car driven home
in falling snow glistens – yours
snuggles under furs

We unlock the door and take our boots off and go in. I keep my coat on, and carry my boots through the house to go out the back and refill the feeders. This weather may be fun for us, but it's no joke for the birds.

pouring hot water
on the glassy bowl – enough
to lift out ice pie

Journey of the Magi

Illuminated Christmas decorations
come in all shapes and sizes:
an inflatable teddy-bear in a red
suit and hood trimmed with white fur,
holding a smaller version of himself
in a front garden on a main road;
other Father Christmases inside
and outside houses, reindeer,
toy trains climbing up stuccoed walls,
sheets of blue lights, sheets of white.
There are whole house-fronts crammed
with clashing colours and odd forms.
You know where you are, driving through
Swansea and Llanelli to Furnace and beyond –
I'm told it's the same in Fordingbridge,
and Sandleheath, and Portland, Oregon –
you're in Santa-Land in December,
after an hour and a half in the car,
and millions of years of evolution.

Ice Cream On A Beach

He kept saying, tilt your head back further,
and I kept thinking, lower the chair then,
till I cottoned on and lifted my chin.
Even then he didn't find it easy,
having to tug this way and that with forceps,
or so he called them, but I couldn't see them,
and thought of them as like my household pliers
with curved blue handles and those grey steel jaws.
From time to time he rested his arms, called
for different instruments, an elevator.
I imagined him levering the tooth out
as I had sweated over that young oak tree
that was in the wrong place by the garden fence.
I could feel movement through the anaesthetic.
But it wasn't painful really, that was
earlier, with the needles going in,
and before that at home, doubled up, moaning,
deciding that snow or not, I had to go.
Now, on a scale of one to ten, he asked,
where is it, seven, eight? Yes, I answered,
ten was when I wished I'd never been born.
I winced and he said, relax, imagine
you're on a beach surrounded by pretty girls,
if you're like me, with a Sidoli's ice-cream.
As I told him when I could speak, I was
thinking about my daughter who has had years
of trouble with bad teeth and painful treatment.
If she can do it you can do it, eh, he said.
Not exactly. I thought of all those times
I'd sat staring at the phone after a call,
trying to feel her pain and wondering

at her courage. How she laughs when we meet.
Good man, said the dentist from time to time,
asking his assistant to keep my head still.
I thought of pictures of four strong men
holding down a patient about to be cut
in the days before modern medicine.
Most of all I kept seeing a piece of string,
one end round a tooth, one tied to a door-knob.

Space Travellers

Ben and Eleanor live in Hinckley now.
Unexpectedly, like visitors from Mars,
they showed up at the door yesterday,
the third Saturday in January,
and sat with us in the warm living room
drinking tea and eating shortcake biscuits
from the tin they had given us for Christmas.
I kept looking at them, large as life, solid,
there in front of us, talking in those voices
that are so familiar, not heard for weeks.
The cold gets in to all kinds of gloves, Ben said,
it will always find a way. When they'd arrived
we'd shaken hands and his had been like ice.
I photographed them as they rode off, waving,
on their brand new bike, all very smart,
distanced inside their astronaut helmets
in the clear but fading late afternoon.
The forecast was frost, and it didn't lie.
At ten they called to tell us they had landed.

Don's Present

For Donald Calway

I'm usually reading and writing first thing, but yesterday I went to catch the post with Don's birthday card so that with luck it would get there on Monday. As I was out, I thought I might as well walk round the village. I was blinking in the unaccustomed sunlight, and my muscles weren't in working order to start with, but I persevered, and the glare eased when I got to the bottom of the hill and, once past the puddle all across the road, turned right opposite Jane's house. There was an unmistakable freshness, being out so early, and the day fine. Thrushes here and there were calling, hardly a song at this time of the year. An unseen horse neighed, beginning in a deep sonar-picture of the depths of its strong body, a vibration like thunder, rising to a falsetto squeal and the gracious grace-notes of the final arpeggio. Not a car passed me, and the dog at the house on the corner didn't bark. By this time I was well breathed, and into my stride. Blackbirds were singing, and robins. The light had the glad expectancy of morning. One of the dogs in the riding-school yard did bark as I passed, but this time none came out and bit me, and in fact only the one was in sight. As I looked I saw a fine display of bright, strutting, picture-book chickens and cockerels, a couple of which hallooed with primal vigour. On the corner where the lanes meet I paused, arrested by an earthy smell of fresh air, mud, and farmyards. With the green fields and the bare trees before me I wondered what memory was begging to be realised. Some sweetness of forgotten life came across, though no label of time or place. I turned down towards home, accepting the sun's brightness gratefully though it still dazzled me. The fine spectacle of massed snowdrops was just as it had been a couple of days earlier, in front of a cottage on the left, and as it is, in fact, every year. I came in, thanking Don for getting me out early on his behalf. This morning I made this, for Don, first thing, in my reading and writing time.

The Pond in the Fields

Which was the moment that seemed an answer
to that intense passage of meditation, a new
insight into familiar thoughts that gave them
a quality of second sight, something amplified,
like rising milk in a pan that overflows,
or the moment when a singer moves and echo
starts to redouble what she has been singing?

Was it when I turned on to that foot-path?
As soon as I did the day came to life.
Grassy banks enclosing trodden earth made it
a little Eden, overhung with trees.
I came to a stile at a pylon's foot
and climbed into a field, and all this seemed
new, though it was only renewed, including
views back over the brow of the green slope.
And on the other side of me, westwards,
a lonely pond I had forgotten about,
nestling in the hollow of the fields, glistened,
mirroring bright sky, so sky and water
seemed not to know which was which, any more
than the tangled branches of a fallen tree
knew which part of them was just reflected
and which was solid wood rising from water,
though agitated ripples wondered whether
breeze or some unseen life was shaking them.

That was the top of the walk, and just then
I saw a wren start from a hedge near me,
and after treading round hardened mud, gaining
the lane with no harm to town shoes, I saw
on the verge in gloom this year's first primroses.
So I'll take that as the moment that answered –
that vision of the gleaming pond between grass
and sky, black branches rising out of it –
that answered my visionary confluence
of familiar thoughts, that Edward Thomas
had died young and been lamented over
as part of that great wave of misery
that engulfed Europe a century ago
and yet had lived on, especially today,
March the third, in the hearts of his readers,
and our minds, our walking bodies, our eyes,
seeing the world with vision he had sharpened –
and then it was he showed me the dew pond
or, as it seemed, touching me for an instant
with his spirit, borrowed me to see with.

Of Chalk and Gold

Chalk, the poems have been saying to me,
chalk, chalk, like an undercurrent, a pulse,
something murmured in a secret language,
but I've been attending to other things
they also say, until I'm about to walk
where he walked a hundred years ago, and read
not only the airy not-nothing-but-something
unsubstantial and elusive, even hidden,
he made of the local habitation
and the name of the place he inhabited,
but against the grain, the poem as map,
and guide, and autobiography.
You take your life in your hands, reading,
since life depends on keeping the spirit
clear and unencumbered and in tune
with what's essential, and poems distil it.
Who would turn chymical gold back to lead?
We hope at least to see where the change happened.

A First Visit to Steep

That morning's news had been of six young soldiers
killed by a roadside bomb in Afghanistan.
From the car I glimpsed the war memorial
with a bouquet of artificial poppies,
perhaps left and renewed all through the year,
or placed there last Saturday or Sunday,
March the third or fourth. Start the walk near the church,
said the guide, and here was the church, but oh,
here were a group of people wearing black,
a young man with a strong, sensitive face
trying not to cry, but not succeeding.
It was as if we had to approach this place
of so much life through the lych-gate of death,
and it seemed fitting that it should be so.

He fell a year short of seeing forty.
Carrying that knowledge lightly as we walked,
I felt his companionship, a young man's,
a young fit man's, as I toiled up the hill
he would have bounded up, no doubt, except
when he was kept in by a twisted ankle
and for the first time turned to writing poems
after a million or so words of prose.
His time was shortened, and so was our walk,
which couldn't do justice to the place. I want
to go back, but it won't be the first time,
with all the specialness of the first time.

Birds sang for the entire two hours, robins,
blackbirds, finches, and above all thrushes,
especially towards the end, and once each
we heard an owl and a drumming woodpecker.
The air is so pure that lichen flourishes
on the bark of trees, and the fallen logs
were covered over with thick, furry moss.
There was a stand of snowdrops at the top
of the hill where we turned along the ridge,
and past The Red House where the poet lived,
as well as in a cottage far below.

The views coming down Shoulder of Mutton Hill
were panoramic, lush, and glorious,
just as the poem 'Wind and Mist' describes.
The memorial is unobtrusive,
dignified. My joints ached, which was my tribute,
like lighting a candle, to put me in tune
with the quotation set into the stone:
and I rose up and knew that I was tired
and continued my journey. Back at the church
the mourners were gone, and I went through the gate.
The outer door of the church looked locked
but wasn't, while the inside door was.
I'll see the Whistler windows another time.
We changed our shoes, drove back to Petersfield,
and on to Storrington to stay with friends.

May Morning in Trerhyngyll

It was five and foggy, May the twenty-third.
The only people I met were in my mind,
a man who lived on Shoulder of Mutton Hill
and a tramp with a rolling run of a gait
who offered him cowslips and watercress.
I thought of my visit to Steep in March
and my surprise, discovering a village
with a name, Oakshott, till then for me attached
only to a stream where the cresses grew.
Now when I read those lines I see again
black lettering on a white fingerpost,
and the Red House's gables among trees.

When I was out this morning all I read
was the hedgerow, scanning pink campion
behind the ranks of delicate cow parsley.
White blossom lined the lane on either side,
and seemed in the fog to float, unanchored.
There were blackbirds and robins singing, an owl,
a thrush, a wren, and later another thrush,
as well as birds I couldn't put a name to,
and a rooster crowed behind a silent barn.

I stopped in the road to look round and listen,
but a blackbird began to sound the alarm,
recognising a member of a species
not to be trusted, so I walked on and heard
a larger animal beyond the hedge
keeping pace and breathing audibly.
I came to where foals and full-grown horses
ambled on grass above me and beside me,
outlined against the misty sky, all
turning their heads to look at me mildly,

observant, open, accepting, gentle.
It was a fine thing to be looked at by them.
The dog that sometimes barks from the garden
of the house on the corner where two lanes meet
must have been dozing somewhere warm indoors.

And so I came round to my home again.
I'd met no-one but a tramp and a poet.
All round the house the singers of May sang still.

Multiverse on the Seine

In this photograph you see both profiles,
her face angled slightly up, half smiling,
but not so broadly that the lips are not
already puckering towards the kiss.
His manifests a masculine restraint,
but seems to be softening and leaning in.

Beside them, one by one, teenagers raised
a hand at chest height in air, a gesture
that made no sense except from the point of view
of a friend taking a picture showing
the top of the tower petted, patted down.
In Pisa they play a similar game, hands
raised to stop the wedding-cake campanile
collapsing in an indeterminate heap.
Galileo's research laboratory
was not further from this just-married pair
than the ebb and flow of tourists who happened
to be there on the same afternoon, and yet
not there, not able to impinge on these two
about-to-merge outlines, this timeless moment.

It's easy to believe in a universe
of eleven dimensions, most of them not
available to our senses, noticing
that juxtaposition of realities each
digitally captured to be harvested
on phones and laptops in two dozen countries
as distant from each other as those people
standing and strolling side by side, all having
the world's most famous landmark to themselves.

The High Garonne

Leaning back against a rock eating salad,
drinking rosé wine, and watching water foam
over multiple rapids in the river,
then gazing at the mountains only just
not high enough to show like those beyond
glimpses of perpetual snow, *la neige*
eternelle, the four of us talking sometimes,
glancing around us at the scenery
and the blond parents with blond children
clambering about and chucking rocks, splash,
into the shallows, all of this was good,
after a stiff walk part of the way up
the hillside among dappled trees and stones.
Just as good was driving on and finding
a place away from other cars and walkers
to lie down in a wood for a siesta
with a paperback novel as a pillow
and feeling as snug as in a bed, asleep
at once, waking stretched out as if growing
at every point up from the earth, seeing
the canopy of pines against the sky,
this was good, yes, it was all very good;
and the view when we stopped again high up
at the Hospice de France, the last building
on the French side of the mountains, where paths
stretched invitingly in two directions
and another stream welcomed other bathers,
with flowers we knew and some we didn't know,
was goodness summed up, spread out like a feast.

Churches in Toulouse

There is a height in stone that seems to rise
above not trouble so much as the meanness
of trouble, its accidental quality.
I thought nothing could transmute my grieving
so well as the lofty Romanesque arches
of the vast Basilica Saint Sernin,
especially the way the semi-circles
spanning the nave are echoed by the glimpsed
smaller arches along the corridored
clerestory, as the rising and falling
of voices must have echoed on all that
labyrinthine stone before winding at last
through the labyrinth of the ear and spirit,
or as water finds ways round and over rocks
in a broad stream in the Pyrenees. I thought
no space could rise above the illusion
of accident, disfiguring sorrow,
so well as those heights – plainchant, mountain, river,
Romanesque – but it's neither the Garonne
I think of today, nor the Basilica;
it's a museum that was once a convent
in the same city, its uncluttered ceiling
delicately crossed at the curved centre
by ribs of gold brought to a focus, crowned
by a single elegant knot like a thought,
a compassionate comprehensive thought
that resolves everything without reaching
for resolution, fusing height with depth,
acceptance altering what will not alter.

Morning in the Parc Lefèvre

After grey streets and lights at the crossing
the sight of an off-white goose through railings
is a transfusion of the almost wild.
The goose looks as solid and as sturdy
as a shire horse motionless in a field,
monumental in September sunlight,
its third dimension super-realised.
Its legs are built for endurance and to heave
that archetypally heavy body
from place to place in search of sustenance.
As it sees me pause beyond the metal bars
it takes three casual web-footed steps
more or less towards me, arches its neck
and slowly opens wide a rubber beak
disclosing red depths with an eloquence
that might mean one of several distinct things
or all of them together – hunger, boredom,
defiance, metaphysical anguish,
or an unshakable affirmative.
I can't help thinking of it as an address,
a greeting even, something no human
stranger in this park is going to offer.
I try a couple of faint smiles at people
shrunk into their scarves against the cold,
provoking terror that I might go further,
and wish somebody a happy new year.
No, for recognition give me that goose,
sharing with an embodied consciousness
not unlike its own the undeniable
fellowship, whatever it means, of being.

Biometric

Put your feet on the yellow shoe-outlines –
that's the easy part. But before that,
open your passport at the photograph
and feed it into this steel-framed slot.
I'm watching the woman in charge but she's
attending to the suspect on her other side.
Because I'm taking my cue from her I fail
to read the instruction next to the machine,
and put the passport in the wrong way up.
I turn it over but still nothing happens.
Now I have the uniform's attention
she feeds it in herself and holds it there
for what seems a long time, till it works, and gates
spring open and I can step forward on to
the yellow circle with the shoe outlines.
Shall I take my glasses off, I ask, doing so.
They're reading glasses and I imagine because
things a few feet away look blurred through them
that the machine would quote see unquote my eyes
blurred as well, though this may not be good optics.
I'm not good for much after that stuffy flight.
The machine with an eye extends, recognising
it's aiming its camera-muzzle at my chest.
That's better – almost eye-level, though not quite.
After watching for some time to see whether
it will do anything else, I notice a sign way off
to my right – the lens is left of ahead –
saying, look here. Where? There? There? Oh, I see,
there. I stare. Earlier this very day
I was looking at my daughter in good light,
and marvelling at the green flecked with brown

of her eyes, something I should like to study,
knowing I don't know when I'll see her again,
possibly not for several long months.
I've no interest in gazing at machines.
Another gate opens and I step through.
You're waiting for me, similarly released.
You laugh. It's so much quicker, isn't it?

III

Flowers in a Terracotta Vase

We heard the teacher's voice before we saw her.
Why do I say I want to *shoo* it away?
If you look very carefully, can you see?
A fuh-*ly*-ee! Yes, a *fly*! Just by listening
we could hear reflected the children's ages,
the way by saying fuh-*ly*-ee she opened
her voice like cupped hands or a flower's chalice.
Now we could see the cross-legged girls and boys
in maroon jumpers looking up at her.
The painting behind her showed crowded colours.
Why, she asked them, are there butterflies?
I noticed a Red Admiral in one place
and a Tortoiseshell in another. Because,
she gathered their murmurs and gave them back,
amplified and enriched, of *pollen*,
the pollen on the flowers, the butterflies
come for *pollen*. Are they like bees, do they make
honey from the pollen? *No*! They *eat* it!
What about the nest under the flowers?
Where is the bird it belongs to? Will it
be able to come back? Why not? Suddenly
these five-year-olds were seeing what Keats saw
on the Grecian Urn, and Szymborska saw
in Hiroshige's people on a bridge,
caught in a sudden downpour: the moment
of the painting stays the same for ever.
Can you see how the nest is made, she asked them.
With twigs, yes, what else, branches, yes, with twigs
and branches, what else can you see? In the nest,
yes, there are eggs, and what do you think might be
inside those eggs, yes, *baby birds*, baby birds.

Do you know what the special word is, she asked,
for baby birds? Put your hands up. One boy
called out and she very gently explained
she didn't want to be mean with all this
handy-uppy thing, but she didn't have eyes
all round her head, only two at the front.
The girl with a raised hand she pointed to
didn't seem less proud, enunciating
the answer, because it had been slipped out
into the consciousness of all of us.
That could be treated as not having happened.
She knew she made it real by how she said it.
It was time for us eaves-droppers to move on.
There were several parties of schoolchildren,
several teachers explaining to them
in the right ways for their different ages
what there was to notice in the pictures.
We'd come back a second day to see them.
How good it was to look at them again,
and good as well to see all the teachers
and their little chicks, all our national treasures.

Woodwork Lesson

For Ken Metcalf

Ken's father was a joiner. In the last year
of his life he taught woodwork at St Dunstan's.
When he died, there were sixteen floral tributes
on the coffin, three from the family,
and thirteen wreaths from the boys at the school.
I remember a man who taught us carpentry
when I was eleven, soft-spoken, taciturn,
with large gentle eyes and a shaven head.
He wore his brown overall with a stoop
from bending over the blade of a chisel
inspecting its edge, showing it to us boys.
There were teachers who got respected, liked,
others who were mocked or criticised.
But we were still only children at heart,
and hadn't hardened ourselves against love
when we found it there, demanding nothing,
this water in the desert, sanctuary
from all the posturing and stridency.
It was like going into a dark stable,
smelling the hay and the warm hidden life.
This was what it might be to do something
with which you had become identified.
Just the way he took a brown pencil,
a special one with an oval section
but otherwise simple, from behind his ear,
peered at the straight edge under his fingertips
to see that it was in exactly the right place,
and then drew a line across the piece of wood
firmly, neither slowly not hastily,

standing next to me and showing me, was one
of the loveliest lessons I ever had.
If he had died I would have sent flowers.
I can see Ken's smile, driving us three times
yesterday and the day before, like last year,
between the town centre and the campus,
me in the front each time, his open face,
telling us this story about his dad.
I expect there's a family resemblance.
In my mind the son, his father, and the man
who taught us woodwork, become one presence.

Casting the Poem

The true poem, I sometimes think, should be
as they say a casting of the I Ching
or the Tarot must, or a horoscope,
a reflection of the universe at that
precise moment in relation to you.
One must come to the poem as naked
and defenceless as a new-born or one dying.
This morning's going to be a crescendo
of urgency about a postponed class
I've had less time than usual to prepare
in which I'll undertake the preposterous
but precise and focused task of guiding less
experienced, not necessarily worse
practitioners to undergo, to submit
to, the uncertainty of poetry
and where it will want to take them, so that
when sitting down to write, and to read first
as a preparation for writing, and even
picking up a pen, they shall not ruin
the poem that is going to startle them
by having guessed correctly in advance
what form it will find or on what subject,
though guessing wrong's integral to the process.

The looming of that rendezvous today
as in a rising sign on the horizon
is a part of the configuration
of planets about this morning's rebirth.
But only part, along with where I was
last week when the students were arriving,
met by a stranger, not who they were used to.

I was on a train in another country
watching for it to move at exactly three,
two o'clock here. The class starts at 2:10.
I thought about them all in the next two hours,
going with my daughter from central Paris
to the *Hotel de Ville* in Livry-Gargan
to collect an emergency passport,
ready at last, leaving us to discuss
if it was too late for her to travel.

And then there is what I supposed, wrongly,
would be my theme when I raised this pencil,
but it belongs here like the sun in Libra:
my shortened walk at lunchtime in the woods,
where I hadn't been for ten days, since leaves
on the path were thin and drab, plastered down
in the mud, with only a few highlights.
What had drawn me forward then was sunshine,
slanting at intervals between trees, striping
the way ahead with inviting brightness.
Yesterday like an unexpected win
a richness of curled and buoyant leaves, piled up
like tempting poppadoms with wavy edges,
yellow and red, big, fresh, abundant,
insisted, though I was being waited for,
I must walk there, I must, and so I did.

The rest of the day having been spent indoors
working away at keyboards, screens, and words,
those crisp sycamore and beech and oak leaves
have the whole of the foreground to themselves,
though last week and this afternoon still shine
in their right places, their houses and their signs.

On the Field of Battle

For Emma Hillier and Bob Walton

Reaching for a word, what was it? Something
I should have found easily but couldn't –
one of those moments that might be, but isn't,
the onset of the winter of the brain,
and the thought has time to surface, calmly,
is this the beginning of the migration
of words like swallows in mid-September,
crowding on telephone wires with outriders
looping the loop until one morning they're gone,
most of them, leaving a few forlorn stragglers?
One day perhaps, that's what it will be, speech
deserting me, as at any age there can be
creative uses of mind one can't quite match
or reproduce from the year before,
going on instead to make something worthwhile
one is only now ripe enough to accomplish.
There is gain and loss, maybe, till the end,
though in some lives, at least to the onlooker,
there seems unambiguous diminution
of powers and capacity for joy.
William Bronk wrote in old age, 'life keeps
hold of me now on *its* terms.' But this was just
one of those false alarms, fire drills, practice
for the day when it really will be time,
perhaps, to evacuate the building,
like Marcus Aurelius reflecting
that when life comes to resemble a hut
in which a smoking fire corrupts the air,
the wise man resolves it is time to go;
a debonair notion of calm control,
which may have its uses on anxious nights

even if, when the crisis arrives, who knows
whether that possibility will occur?
But these are thoughts of gaiety today,
a flexing of mental fingers, the morning
after two absorbing conversations
with like-minded *literati,* allowing
and obliging me to command coherent
passages of improvised speech, and reach
for words and combinations of words, stiff
like muscles rejoicing in the first good stretch
for weeks of a walk up and down the cliffs.
I had been speaking about Robert Creeley,
his quivering, fraught, fragmentary poems
making it a comical surprise to learn
that as letter-writer, teacher, essayist,
he was unusually… here I paused,
an everyday word eluding me, and felt
in the wait like what's-his-name just before
the great battle he doesn't want to fight –
Arjuna – with Krishna delivering
the entire *Bhagavad Gita* to him,
asking to behold his immortal form,
seeing an infinite number of faces,
ornamented by heavenly jewels,
displaying overwhelming miracles,
until out of pity Krishna resumes
his ordinary human camouflage.
Such was the moment of fullness, of wealth,
of life's hurrying energies in which
I paused and became conscious, and rejoiced,
waiting till the word I wanted came
and the onrush could continue. I relished
the interval till it did, knew myself
to be alive and glad of it, and then
the word I needed arrived: *articulate.*

The Nest On The Ledge

Every day when I go to my office I put my head against the glass and peer at a window-ledge on the floor below. The mistle thrush is still on her nest. If I take up the small binoculars I've left there just for her sake I see her wide eye, vigilant, seeing me. She's been there weeks now. I must ask someone who knows how long it takes from beginning to brood, to hatching, to flight. Leaving at half past seven last night I saw a thrush and a magpie standing near each other, confronting. A large thrush, a mistle thrush, standing her ground. We were, I suppose, all conscious of the untidy bundle of twigs and grass, hidden in plain sight in the corner of one of many identical windows in rows above us. I took a few steps towards them and the thrush didn't budge but the magpie flew off out of sight, the long diagonal across the car park. I turned towards my car, unlocked it. It was a minor victory, but I knew the magpie would be back.

★

The thrush was on the nest all right when I had my first look for two days, but she wasn't just sitting. She seemed to be treading something down rhythmically, pummelling something like a bread-maker. I got ready for my last two-hour class and gave it. I discovered more things they didn't know – sea-shanties, folk-songs, Shenandoah, the Greek for Bacchus; who Ariadne, Titian, and Kabir were. What shocked me was Shenandoah, the rest I expected. I promised to write them all references. Back in my office I went through work by one of them with her for another hour. Afterwards I trained my binoculars on the nest. Was that thing a living thing? Yes. It moved, but it was indistinct. Something that might be a leg. Was there one of it or more than one? Suddenly, out of nowhere, there was the thrush, big and sharply focused, with a worm; and there were two beaks stretched so wide you'd think it must hurt, open mouths dwarfing the rest of the heads with what looked like the eyes screwed shut. The open mouths were on strong necks and came up – this was the thing – absolutely vertical, not aslant. The parent bird dipped into each, and cocked her beady eye and clocked me, and flew off to get more food. The nest became indistinct again in the fading light. I must take in some more powerful field glasses and the camera. It will be days before I'm there again. I hope they'll live. And the students, with so much to learn, I wish them well in a dangerous world. I noticed the fresh green leaves on the birch between me and the nest, so delicate, unspoiled.

The Mug In The Common Room

When I need tea I go to the common room
and there's a couple who are often there.
He's always pleased to see me and he talks,
and I talk back, ask him polite questions
and, when prompted, reminisce. He's amazed
at the famous speaker I invited here –
it comes up because we've discussed his books.
I try to draw her into conversation
and get one-word answers. She might be appalled
to think she gives this impression, but the more
I talk with her friend and the happier
he seems, the more disapproving she looks.

It may be just my imagination.

Or the picture she's getting of who I am
from my stories of old times and my jokes.

My appearance.

                    Dammit, my very essence
must be obnoxious to her, the more so
the more I make a prat of myself. But how
can I stop when the young man is pleased
to have an older ally in this place?

If they both had the same attitude
I'd know what to do. I would clear out fast,
or put more coins in the honesty box
and press the buttons for another tea.

As it is I drink the one I've bought, there,
instead of taking it back to my office,
and remember uneasily afterwards
that I left the cardboard mug, not quite empty,
for somebody else to tut and clear away.

A Good Home

She was smiling from the start, almost speechless,
gradually more able to respond
to our cheerfulness and our reminders.
Our acted-out brightness didn't feel false,
just the appropriate way of being,
like a whole-body wave from side to side
painting the sky, so as to be seen
by someone on a hilltop opposite.
Transfixed by my part in the pantomime
a neat elderly gentleman, looking well,
stood in the spacious, bright refectory
a few feet away, framed by a high arch,
seeming, I thought, wistful, as if excluded,
and wanting to join in. I smiled at him,
not really surprised when his expression
didn't change. That questioning blankness
must have become his permanent address.
We carried on warming our friend to life,
and her smiles crested as laughter. Friends' names,
more than half forgotten, triumphed in her mouth.
A motherly nurse came and spoke with us.
Another approached the melancholy man,
asked him if he'd like to sit down and led him
patiently to a table behind me.
Meanwhile our conversation was ending.
It was time to go, but we left uplifted –
our friend was being so well looked after.
It's true that she won't stay that stimulated.
The most normally intelligent thing she said
was when we first arrived and asked her whether
we could sit with her a while. She laughed. All day!

Phil Says

for Phil Pearson

I don't know if you know, Phil says, they're mixed,
the wards, and if you're over sixty you're in
with the geriatrics. It's not attractive.
They find you a bed wherever they can.
The widow who lives in the cul-de-sac
in the village under the power lines
he says, was in the maternity unit.
Phil made friends with a man on the same ward
and went to talk to him at two a.m. –
since everyone was awake, why not, he thought –
and he seemed fine. Later a nurse appeared,
and looked at him and shouted, help, says Phil,
and then the runners (as I call them) came,
two who looked as if they wouldn't be able
to lift anyone, then two who could, and put
screens around his bed, and then they put, he says,
screens around *my* bed, and in the morning
they said, oh, didn't you know? He passed away
during the night. In a ward with six beds,
in the five days Phil was there, three patients died.
You have to tell your visitors not to be
too raucous, *you* know, because if relatives
were making their last visit to someone
they wouldn't want that going on round them.
When the staff decided Phil should go home
he said Julia would have to bring his clothes,
but they wouldn't wait, and he felt foolish,
walking corridors in bright pyjamas,
frayed slippers, and a homely dressing gown.

Phil's voice down the line sounds faint to start with
but gets more like himself as he talks on.
One time he had had a coughing spasm
and had passed out, and the doctors wanted tests,
convinced he had had a fit, and he thought,
oh no, another year without driving,
but as he'd thought, he hadn't, the scans were clear.
There's a great deal more Phil tells me. It is all
interesting, and some of it is funny.
Quite a lot of it is bloody frightening.

Prisoners

I sit surrounded by people who all seem
iller than I think I am, older, or both.
A man passes us slowly with a stick,
his face expressionless with resignation,
and no one else is much more animated.
We are like stones or single-celled beings
dimly lit by stirrings of consciousness,
struggling to break free from limitation
but more imprisoned as our weakness grows,
captured in a war our side is losing.
We, the disgraced, are smiled on from the wall
by a framed picture of a blonde young woman,
bare-shouldered, in a shiny dark-blue dress.
A man older than me is sent by a nurse
behind a curtain to take off his trousers.
He comes back with a box holding his clothes,
wearing a standard purple gown, and sits
ready to have his anonymity
stripped from him when it's his turn to stand up.
I'm allowed to stay as I came. I shall just
have to pull my shirt off and press my chest
against a cold glass window and breathe in.
A woman has to do as the man did:
the nurse murmurs the words bra and knickers.
She too comes out and sits waiting, calmly
and with dignity, for her name to be called.
On the side of a box on a trolley
I see chalked the letters P.O.W.

Witness

When he told her she would have
to go to a station for questioning,
a different station from the one
they had taken her husband to,
he added, are you happy with that?
No, she answered, I'm not happy,
but I am willing. In the bare room
he asked again, are you happy with that,
and got the same answer, and again,
till finally he corrected himself,
no, you're not happy, are you?
Then he smiled, and she said,
thank you for smiling at me.
He said, I do that sometimes,
and that was as human as it got.

Dannie

Late at night, on a screen, the news, a pang.
A year ago almost to the day he was
the last and wittiest and alas the briefest
speaker after his own birthday dinner.
That was the last time I set eyes on him.
There were many of us and where I was sitting
I couldn't say hello or shake his hand,
but when he rose to thank his well-wishers
and he looked speakingly at me, I knew
he recognised me and knew all about me
and would, as I would, have wanted to have
the conversation we had barely started.
I hoped till Sunday night we still might have it,
perhaps in the favourite London café
he wrote about in his most recent books,
or Ogmore where he lived and I take children
and friends to bathe or walk by the water.
This morning I retrieve from a high shelf
double-stacked behind more recent volumes
the old *New and Collected* and start reading,
moving between the younger and the older.
I underline a word I'll have to google.
Yes, that's one of his hall-marks, and the wit.
The doctor's and the Jew's unflinching look
into the darkness of the soul and body,
the defiant playfulness and ego,
no bones made about desire or anger,
and the spade of history and holocaust
called an unvarnished spade, though artfully.
Above all how full of energy, how full
of him his printed words are now he's stilled.

It's as if at the moment of passing
the poet's life migrates into his poems.
As he was leaving the restaurant I touched him
to hand him with a few sheepish words
a birthday card that we had written for him.
He turned with his overcoat half on
and took it with no words but such another
speaking look as beats most eloquence.
I feel his eyes on me, reading his poems.

The Land Has Its Say

For Henry Lyman

Henry has composed not just a poem
but a book of poems, each poem tugged
into a dense warp and woof like the seats
of the stool and the heavy oak-legged bench
my mother wove of corn-coloured strands
twisted so tight that though formed of stuff
which had grown out of earth and could unravel
they were as strong as steel and wouldn't give.
Each of Henry's poems is made like that.
You can prod it and trust your weight to it
and it will yield a bit but won't give way.
You might pull at an end here and there, thinking
to unpick it, reconfigure something.
Go on, try. You will learn that every line,
every taut hawser of natural fibre
is exactly as and where it needs to be.
The individual poems are woven
just as firmly and securely into
an architecture that grows inside you,
lifting you into a meditation
that is high and deep and goes on echoing
something indeterminate and infinite
at the centre of a structure, like its parts,
so beyond second guessing you think that though
it hasn't always been there it should have been.

Letter to Jack Gilbert

I think of a man aged eighty who has put
his life into poetry. I mean, he writes
about his life, and poetry's what he lives
for. Up close to his poems, you get him –
tall, sinewy, sunburnt, working first in
factories, then in fields on a Greek island.
You get the story of the wife who left him
but remained his friend, of the other wife
who died, the way he goes on loving both, how
he nearly died himself, falling through a tree.
His poetry fills the world, reaches from earth
to sky, the zenith from which Icarus
in one of his poems falls, not failing,
'just coming to the end of his triumph.'
Poetry fills the world when you're close to it,
but you step back and it becomes ghostly.
Where you could smell the man's or woman's scent,
feel the compact muscular presence, like
a leopard ready to spring, there's a whisper,
a reduced two-dimensional image, beard,
roll-neck jumper, aging face. The obverse
of Rilke's praise of Orpheus, 'all singing
is him.' On each reading I think, what's that rose
doing in the poem? – 'Only let the rose
every year bloom at its pleasure. It is
Orpheus. We should not trouble about
other names.' And then the image unfolds
as it fades: 'Is it not already much
if he overstays by a few days sometimes
the bowl of roses?' Wallace Stevens wrote
in 'The Planet on the Table': 'Ariel

was glad he had written his poems,' then:
'It was not important that they survive.'
Jack, let's be glad it was given us to sing,
even if, from a few feet away, all
that can be seen is a caricature,
like shrivelled roses. We shall have kissed the joy
as it flew, we will have soared with Icarus,
triumphant till we dived into the water.

The Last Hamlet of Words

For Carol Rhodes, painter

I went into a dozen bookshops in Hay,
that town for the cognoscenti of tomes.
I bought *The Poet's Tongue*, edited by
W H Auden and John Garrett,
another anthology edited
by Tony Frazer, and *Selected Poems*
by Ungaretti, with facing translations
by Andrew Frisardi. I nearly bought
Book Three of Ronald Duncan's five-book epic
Man, because I'd admired extracts from Book Two.
If I had seen a Roethke I'd have got it,
because of one poem of his reproduced
in Ted Hughes's *Poetry in the Making*
which I really like, though other poems
I've found by him have disappointed me.
We drove home and I nipped out again for bread
and dropped in at a charity shop and found
a thing I'd seen years before, easy to laugh
or cringe at, edited by Mary Wilson,
My Favourite Poem chosen by big names,
the poems often extracts, none with details
beyond the poet's name. Half of them I knew.
I stood there reading and glancing through, and put
the book back on the shelf and left the shop
and carried on walking around the town,
but there had been this passage by Rilke
without any clue as to where it was from.
'Exposed on the heart's mountains,' it begins, 'look,
how small there! Look, the last hamlet of words, and

higher, (but still how small!) yet one remaining
farmstead of feeling: d'you see it?' Well, I had
to have that, and when I passed the shop again
I surprised a man looking at novels
by reaching past him and removing neatly
the slim, dog-eared paperback from the pile
I'd left it on the top of. There are other things –
a de la Mare and a passage from Byron
I didn't recognise. Of course, I've got their
Complete Poems, but I shall find these things
more readily in this book. You have to be
of a certain age to remember how
Private Eye mocked Mary Wilson and her verse,
what a joke she became. You don't have to
have much sophistication to see how naff
this concoction is. You have to have the nerve
to find Cinderella among the ashes,
and bear her away with you because her foot
fits the glass slipper you have always with you.
The Rilke was chosen by Prue Leith. All
royalties went to a leukaemia trust.
I paid 75p to Tenovus,
the cancer charity, on Cowbridge High Street,
and went home to the hamlet of Trerhyngyll.

IV

Visions of Llandaff

1: Words Inside a Birthday Card

If you go down the path between the cathedral
and the steep Dean's Steps up to the green,
you come to two stiles, and can go three ways:
left beside the retaining wall under limes;
right, into the lush churchyard with yew trees
circled by low walls and leaning crosses;
or straight ahead between a playing field
and a wild-flower meadow towards the river.

If you go to the river there are more choices:
left or right, on or over the embankment.
I didn't scramble down, as I sometimes do,
to skim stones across the water and watch
and slow down enough to appreciate
the life of the mallards swimming, flying,
shaking themselves vigorously, diving.
Time was short today, I was stiff, I was cold,
three reasons not to stop but to keep moving.

I went on without regret, getting warmer,
on one of the parallel paths towards the weir,
but I hadn't gone far before I stopped to hear
a robin singing, and going on singing,
and I leaned back to look right up, and yes,
there he was near the top of a lone tree,
and I watched and went on listening and heard
as well as the robin other birds singing,
and the river overcoming all resistance,
and looked around me as the birds sang on
and the air in this enclosed spot warmed me,
the chilly north-west breeze screened out.

I saw insects all of one sort, halfway
to wasps in size but softer, quieter,
like a ladder of angels ascending
and descending beside the robin's tall tree,
and thought how easy it is to ignore
insects because we don't approve of them,
but felt how welcome these were here
as part of the livingness of the world.

And the same with young sycamore growth,
so often a nuisance in the wrong place,
but here were young sycamore leaves opening,
which I've watched progress at intervals from
bare branches to points to furry buds to this
in recent weeks, leaves open and opening,
not yet full-sized and more russet than green,
and suspended among them were these fine
mobiles of generation apparatus,
and giving time to taking all this in
changed me, I'd been impatient and depressed,
but that all fell off me while I was there.

I walked slowly onwards to the weir
with gulls in a row all along the top,
sometimes taking off singly on spread wings
to circle and fly around and land again.
There was a crouching heron here as well,
not moving. I watched, herons being neither
rare nor common in this place, but I couldn't
wait any longer for it to do something,
and I saw how open-air life goes on,
both quick and alert and far slower than I
could stand, birds with their brief lives, their long days,
enduring from one cold sunrise to the next.
I had only an hour to spend among them
between one appointment and three others,
so I went back up to the cathedral
where I chose this card and lit a candle.

2: A Lost View

There's a view at Llandaff I've carried with me
for years wondering if I made it up, because
every time I go I look for and can't see it.
I stand at the top of the path that leads
down the hill past the cathedral's west door
looking towards the river and what I see
is lovely but it's not what I remember.

Yesterday thinking wearing my best trousers
might prevent me getting further than the stile
at the bottom of the hill because of mud,
I decided to do the fripperies instead
of marching straight down intent on water,
and I climbed the little mound with fallen stone
and a dainty path round the stone which leads
nowhere and doesn't look interesting
which is why I haven't climbed it for ages
and oh! there it was at last, my lost view,
with the west front three-quarter face
below me in the hollow and towering
literally above me with its northern spire
overtopping the tower in the south corner,
and a glimpse of rural hills beyond, one
of which must be Caerphilly Mountain,
its pass guarded by the Traveller's Rest –
starting point for many a bygone walk.

Then I walked down the hill and realised
I tend to forget there's a metalled path now
across the meadow where I once saw fox-cubs
at dawn and often see groups of magpies
so I was able to go on, thinking I'd have to stop

when I got to the river, but I also forgot
there's a good path on the raised embankment,
and I thought of Shelley writing I always
go on until I am stopped, full-stop, and I never
am stopped, full-stop, and I saw that the path
down from the embankment to the place
where once the pebbles I spun across the water
made rainbows with the drops they centrifuged
was actually fairly firm and dry,
and I thought I am not going to go there
surely, but oh, here I am doing it.
I didn't go to the edge and didn't mind.
The stones were mostly covered by the high Taff,
swollen with global warming and on speed.

So I walked on to the glorious weir
where the white water does its imitation
of Victoria Falls or Niagara.
I thought I'd have to go back the same way
because of mud – my best trousers again –
but I was able to step round puddled earth
and do the circuit, following the path
under the retaining wall below the woods.
I was back near the stile before I knew it,
because my mind was full of happy thoughts.
All the time I was walking the sun shone,
and I couldn't remember feeling so well,
and I waved my arms about and sang
and made inarticulate sounds of joy.

I went into the cathedral and bought cards
and presents and had a laugh with the nice
grey-haired lady who wouldn't charge me
for one little booklet that wasn't priced,

so I said I'd put two pounds in the box,
but took back from the counter the 10p
I'd replaced with two 5s just before
she took the lot, and I said, fair's fair,
which was when we laughed, and I just
had time to go and find the reliefs
of the Six Days of Creation by Burne-Jones
I'd found on a postcard but never seen
before, either on a card or *in situ*,
though I've been coming here so many years.

3: Visions of Llandaff

Summer rain on leaves and old stone.
Nobody about. I'm seeing things,
but more than seeing is the feeling –
the way the permeation of water
through air under tall trees and taller spire
creates a soft fellowship in which things
bloom and are tenderly magnified,
stone and lichen on stone, ivy leaves,
daisy-like erigeron on the low wall
where the grass slopes from the lych-gate sharply down
to the high south side of the cathedral
with the dog-tooth semi-circle round the door.
It's that feeling that was offered me
and which I only partially received,
allowing myself to be distracted by
looking and by looking for camera angles.
I rerun the walk in thought to gather up
that vision like the fragments of Osiris.

I remember an intense early version
of this transfiguring, lonely, sixteen,
less lonely for being alone for once,
walking around the old castle at Wertheim
surrounded by tall trees and a soft rain,
a squirrel the one other unrooted thing.

I move down past the cathedral to where
the paths all meet and the ground levels out.
There's a large muddy pool under the wall
on the path that leads to the wide weir,
which must be a foaming cataract today.
The path straight ahead across the field

is surrounded by angelica's white umbels,
tall as a man and dense and dishevelled,
pearled and magnified with shining rain.
In the churchyard an old grey cross leans
just visible through rosebay willow-herb,
taller than a man, in purple bloom.

The elegant gold cockerel on the spire
is so high, the eye reaching to sight it
needs to reach again to encompass it.
Even inside the cathedral I see
more than I usually see, the wood
and furnishings of the pulpit, Epstein's
huge Christ that divides the nave into two.
For once I don't just see, I register this
incarnation of the divine as human,
standing stiffly in straight, encasing robes,
head raised to heaven, strong hands by his sides
open and facing forwards. I see the knight
on the marble tomb beside his pious wife
with the French poodle at his stony feet.
I linger longest at the small carving
in wood from 1430 of a nun
in a raised sloping bed, half upright,
surrounded by bearded men with hollow,
kind, and holy faces, meant to be
the Virgin being read to by Saint Peter.

Outside again, I see how beautiful
the rain is now, dancing on the brown slabs
of paving stones in front of the Dean's Steps,
leading up under trees and then obscured.
I cross their glistening sheen and then turn left
up the steep path under more trees,

feeling the rain and crowding presences
of so many and such different plants, masses
of luxuriant wet growth, and think again
of Hopkins' lines, 'let them be left, O let them
be left, wildness and wet; long live the weeds
and the wilderness yet,' and feel I have,
for all my inattention, completed something.

★

I look through yesterday at the day before
and still see first the honey-coloured stone
of the square tower as I tilt my head

to see it outlined on cloud to the top.
I see the sculptured group from 1430
and realise Saint Peter would not have read

to Mary dying. What could a book tell them
better than what Jesus whom they knew
had said, of which they needed no reminding?

But I love the carving's truth to the time
in which it was made, the sweetness of the faces
of the monks pretending to be early saints.

★

I almost prefer Llandaff in the rain.
The emblematic glow on my retina
on Thursday at waking had the warm colour
of the stone on the cathedral spire,
taking precedence over all of Wednesday.
At noon yesterday I looked up again

at that stone spire and saw how its power came
from blending several colours, yellow and brown
being interspersed with red and white and grey.
But this morning the presence that centred
my meditation was still from Tuesday –
the tall blooms, purple and white, concealing
a slanting dark cross on an ancient tomb,
enveloped in an atmosphere condensed
into a myriad drops as tender
as the Schumann song I heard a tenor singing
this morning as I moved about the kitchen.
That the cross leaned and was half-hidden
was not a bitter commentary on grief
and the futility of memorials,
but an image of a reconciling
of our lives, remembered and forgotten, with
the perennial beauty of wild flowers,
so fresh, new every year, shining with rain.

V

Attic Interlude

1: Homage To Clio

We have arrived and not arrived, slept late
and not dared open the shutters yet, although
the sun was bright on patterned kitchen tiles
I crossed to find a teapot with a strainer.
Our travel-day passed in a blur and seems
fuzzy in memory. I am trying
to bring Clio into sharper focus,
who made us so welcome and had already
explained so much to the others in the hour
before we stood on the step, ready to knock.
Thomas opened to us, then Alison came,
both of them taller and stronger since Christmas,
and there was Clio, recognisable
from her picture, with Jean-Paul and Cathy.
Freshly pressed orange juice in a tall glass,
a tasty home-baked snack like a samosa
in a paper napkin, and such a warmth
of generous feeling as magicked away
all the exhaustion, stress, and dust of journeys.
I felt I had to stop myself exclaiming
at the beauty of the house with all its things,
its lovely details and its spaciousness,
for fear the repetition might be tiresome.
It's a place evidently loved and lived-in.

Clio will stay at her mother's for the week.
She left us a magnificent huge bowl
Of *choriatiki* and some chilled Greek wine.
She is a teacher, speaks perfect French, studied
in Paris where her daughter is a lawyer.
Photos surround us: them at different ages.
The last twenty and more years pass before us.
What move me as much are the well-worn books
cramming the shelves, French classics, modern thinkers:
a devoted life of love and study.
As the week goes by I shall get to know
Clio better and better by osmosis,
absorbing who she is from her surroundings,
but see her again only when we're leaving
to give the keys back and say goodbye. Would we
in different circumstances become friends,
finding common ground despite lacunae
in my knowledge of our common culture?
My Francophile father would have loved her,
and this house, and our dawning adventure.

But time goes on, though the children are still
quiet, absorbed, gazing at little screens,
and the parents too are keeping low profiles.
Let the day begin. Welcome to Athens.

2: Finding Our Way

Turning left out of Clio's house and right
along a street of fragrant orange trees
we find ourselves in no time in a park,
somewhere unfenced and full of cypresses
with flowering shrubs and paths of marble,
cobblestones *in excelcis* and historic,
climbing and winding, winding on and climbing,
cold in the shade but hot in the bright sun.
Pausing, we see the city fall below us,
with mountains girdling it except just there -
that horizontal strip of distant glimmer -
is it? It is, the sea, and that's a tanker
or some cargo ship, and there's another.
This is the Hill of the Muses, a sign says,
confirming we are where we think we are.
A little rustic church appears suddenly,
closed, emanating charm and peacefulness,
with crosses in the patterns on the doors
and patterns in the brickwork like small steeples.
We have climbed fairly high to get this far,
but above the church steps rise to an arbour
with a vine roofing a framework of rafters,
and a bicycle leaning against a bench.
I see no lock on it and looking higher
to the side I see half-concealed a woman
of student age lying on another bench,
knees raised and head raised, reading a paperback.
Whatever else there may be in her life
this must be something marvellous to do.
I go back down without undue hurry,
or exaggerated quietness, no need,
and see and catch up with my five companions,

walking on all more or less together,
distancing ourselves from time to time to look
at something near or far that has intrigued us.
It's good to be here, without expecting
to find ourselves, as we suddenly do,
gazing right up at the Acropolis.

3: The Erechtheion

We follow the multilingual gaggle
of teenagers and other tourists round
the track that circles the huge monument
to the right, all of us trying to see it
with wonder and delight, as we know we should.
It certainly has location, location,
going for it and again location,
crowning the sacred rock above the city
and the bay with the workaday trading ships,
dieseling rather than steaming these days
to and from Piraeus round the headland.
But as we trudge along the Parthenon's
blank south flank of hefty, muscled pillars
(try objecting to our rightful dominance,
they seem to say) we notice on our left –
I murmur to myself and a stranger
smiles at me in recognition, knowing
that's what those figures are – 'caryatids',
four weathered matrons in brown honey stone,
with graceful damp-fold drapery all round them,
supporting on their heads like water pitchers
the capitals below the pediment.
We detour to the west face of the temple
and feel that *frisson* when the sleeping spirit
rises and opens, all the dust and tensions
of its day and its own imperfections
falling from it in the contemplation
of this portico with fluted pillars,
moth-eaten by the ages at the edges,
neither feeble nor brutal in proportion
to the whole shape, from steps to broken cornice.
Later in the Acropolis museum

I read that this and not the Parthenon
was the most ancient site of ritual,
sacred to Poseidon and Athena,
named after her Gaia-fostered son, produced,
like Jesus, by parthenogenesis,
not from the Holy Ghost but from the semen
of the thwarted Hephaestus on her thigh.
Out of attempted rapes and ravishment –
the battle of the Lapiths and Centaurs
commemorated on the ancient friezes
of the Parthenon and other temples grew
from the excited horse-men trying to force
the Lapith women – the Athenians
made objects that transcend their origins,
and still surprise us into the sublime.

4: The Changing Of The Guard

Before I can see anything else again
from yesterday I have to acknowledge
the image of soldiers in their fancy dress
standing outside the blank-faced parliament
from inside which there was no sign of life
except one man in a suit opening
a door on a long balcony, coming out,
leaning forward, carrying a brief-case,
and disappearing again into darkness,
perhaps to find his way to a car-park
underground and so out of the building.
The country's fate is being discussed, if not
determined, in Riga with all of Europe,
almost, in between there and here, presidents,
prime ministers, and finance ministers
agreeing that time is running out and still
a deal seems no nearer being struck. Now
the central government has demanded
local councils empty their coffers and give
all their contingency reserves to it,
to keep the wheels turning another week.
The councillors have expressed their anger.
Foreigners make disapproving noises
and shake their heads in disbelief about
the chances of Greece meeting conditions
for the next tranche of the bailout money.

Meanwhile the young man in the ticket office
on the Acropolis with a haunted look,
as hatchet-faced as the economist turned
statesman but without his coolness under fire
and battle-hardened charisma tells me

he can't accept the card I offer him,
and seeing me incredulous looks me
in the eyes and says, 'lack of bank support,'
like a cornered animal or a martyr
with a martyr's dignity, and I nod,
as Dante nods acknowledgement in hell,
and pay cash with no further argument,
which still for the time being means euros.

Now, here, with other tourists the six of us
await the arrival of the minute hand
on the twelve, and watch the soldiers chosen
for their height and good looks dressed in short skirts
with white stockings that make their long legs seem
as if moulded in porcelain, and pompoms
on their shoes, stand a long time motionless,
then do a strange dance, slow, with elements
of tai chi, goose-stepping and stately ballroom,
to be replaced by soldiers not so tall,
still well over six foot, and disappear
at a march with an escort in khaki
through the crowd, round the corner, out of sight
back to barracks, while the imposing façade
of the parliament building gives away
nothing of what anyone in there knows,
and I'm left this morning thinking nothing
could trump the way the soldiers in white stockings
and bedroom slippers with studs on the soles
and steel horseshoes on the heels lifted them up
repeatedly to show us and then stamped;
but I'm also seeing a man with neat hair
leaning forward, wearing a well-cut suit,
glimpsed high on the outside of the building,
wondering what he knows and fairly certain

that whatever it is there's almost nothing
he can do about it here on one edge
of Europe, while at the opposite end
time runs out, and on to some conclusion.

5: Good Faith In Athens

The waiter always acted like a person
as well as being perfectly a waiter,
discreet and helpful, not disappearing
into his role like the one observed by Sartre,
given as an example of bad faith.
We lingered over lunch in sun and shade
after our strenuous morning travelling
on foot and by metro across Athens
and walking round the museum looking
at statues of draped women and nude men,
Archaic, Classical and Hellenistic,
together with the bronze of Zeus or Neptune,
arms outstretched and larger than life, flinging
an absent thunderbolt, if it is Zeus,
or holding a trident and a dolphin's tail.
Just when we thought we had seen everything
we found ourselves in front of the gold mask
from Mycenae that may not really be
Agamemnon's, as Schliemann thought it was,
but is a very striking older man
of chiselled face, severe but sensitive.
We drained our welcome glasses of house wine.

The waiter came at a glance to bring the bill.
We haven't got a card machine, he lied,
nobly, for the dignity of his country.
We praised the meal sincerely, and his service.
He thanked us for our kindness and we wished
his people well, and that started him talking.
When I mentioned a name he made the point
that finance ministers in other countries
were lawyers, not economists like Greece's.

But now the government was borrowing –
I was keen to show I was keeping up –
from the local councils, I interrupted.
Yes, he said, and this is the phrase I hear
in his excellent English with a slight,
solemn accent, and I hope it is not true,
but it is rumoured, from the hospitals.
All our expressions of solidarity
fell to the ground, accepted as well-meant
but as light trash in the face of something
being lived daily by the families
of helpful men and women we encounter.
I see the waiter's face, but won't describe it:
people of good faith deserve discretion.

We walked off lunch heading through noisy streets,
crowded with cars and Greeks about their business,
to the museum of Byzantine art,
where beauty has migrated from the body
to gold mosaics and to solemn haloes
around the heads of saints and saintly donors,
and Christ Pantocrator, He Who Rules All,
or doesn't, and the Virgin of Tenderness.

6: Vision On The Muses' Hill

One might have thought of sight, but who could think
Of what it sees, for all the ill it sees?
Wallace Stevens, 'Esthétique du Mal'

Once every holiday my daughter decides
the moment has come for some portrait shots.
In evening light on the Hill of the Muses
yesterday she asked me to stop right there,
and after I had posed self-consciously
suggested I might try being natural
or thinking poetic thoughts, reciting.
I was surprised by the Muses' choice, the words
I heard myself start to pronounce, not sure
I'd get to the end of them without stumbling,
Milton's sonnet on his blindness, and then
as a pendant and in lighter mood, Wordsworth's
'my heart leaps up when I behold/ A rainbow
in the sky.' Again, I wasn't certain
I wouldn't falter, and again I didn't.
Both poems came out of deep places, in me,
and in their authors, and in the place we were.
I had been meditating on my own
limitations and frustrations, like Milton,
but seeing how in a larger perspective
there is an effort of acceptance needed
by all of us to make terms with discontent.
'They also serve...' And however thwarted
we feel, we should never lose our wonder:
coming out of the Byzantine museum
we had seen a rainbow unexpectedly
the day before over the hills round Athens.
And now here I was on the Muses' Hill,

close to the Areopagus which had been
the high court of appeal for civil justice
in the city thought of as the origin
of a whole tradition we too inherit.
Milton had been in my mind already
because he wrote a defence of freedom
entitled *Aereopagitica.*
Between the Olympic stadium below
and the Parthenon there on the other hill,
coming down from the summit of the Muses,
two of our greats spoke through me with their passion,
their *gravitas* and awareness of life's
mystery and meaning, and each one praised,
where the flowers and grasses and olive trees
as well as the panoramic views all round
made the gift of vision such a blessing,
the privilege, lost or preserved, of seeing.

7: The Temple Of Hephaestus

Unexpectedly, after shopping and crowds,
on a hill the temple of Hephaestus,
the completest example of its kind,
most of its frieze intact and vivid still,
imposing but less heavy-spirited
than the Parthenon, like the Erechtheion,
a touch more masculine as you'd expect,
and benefitting from its isolation
among the ruins of the Agora –
I see it, honey-brown on the bright sky,
and savour it before it vanishes
into the ruck and jumble of impressions.

8: Selfie As An Ancient Ruin

I'm having my first sea-bathe of the year,
and it's still April. The water's chilly
even here somewhere on the Aegean
between Athens and the southern limit
of the mainland where we have just admired
the dazzling white marble pillars of the now
roofless temple of Poseidon against
a brilliant deep azure afternoon,
and seen the blue intensified again
looking over the edge of the headland
into the sea and at the speckled mountains
all round the horizon and the islands.
Now we've driven up the other coast-line
and found this almost deserted shingle beach
where the children and I wince at the cold
but inch our way in and it's so calm, so clear,
I find myself swimming further than I do
when the sea's rough or I'm swamped by breakers,
able to breathe in between steady strokes
and put my head back down and move forward
watching the rocks and sand through trusty goggles.
Afterwards I look round the bay and see
everything with a renewed clarity –
the rocks and the sparse green on the hillside,
an occasional house, some purple flowers.
This is all right, I think, a bit more of this,
walking miles each day, swimming in the sea,
and not quite so much wine in the evenings,
and I'd get younger because healthier,
even while Alison and Thomas grow up
visibly in front of my eyes. Of course
I know I can't really do that, repeating

as I do whenever I have such thoughts
my favourite line from Samuel Johnson,
'Nor think the Doom of Man reversed for thee.'
All the same it is a shock, hours later,
to see the picture Cathy took of me
in the water, lips pursed as if whistling,
probably from the cold or a sharp stone,
and with my hair no longer merely grey
but shining silver as I've never seen it -
the sun on glistening salt and salty water
must have helped. Below the neck I'm hidden,
with just a swirl of white in front of me
like the tail and body of a merman.
Cathy has a better interpretation:
doesn't *Papi* make a good Poseidon?
Well, if we must age, let us do it as gods.

9: What We Shall Take With Us

The deep, deep red of the poppies growing
wild on Philopappos Hill, abundant
but not invasive little groups here and there
among the wild oats and the feathered grass,
long burrs the colour of ripening corn.
Those wild oats, high and dense and Nordic-blonde,
soft straight tresses pearled with softer seed-heads.
The olive trees along the winding paths
and the avenues with foot-worn marble flags.
The cypress trees, some with tall spires, the leaves
like little hands holding out dark bobbles.
The way after a week of walking here
some parts of it have become familiar
but the whole place is extensive enough,
maze-like enough, that we can still get lost
or hesitate at points we should recognise
where four or five directions all beckon.
The sudden views of the modern city
below us, ringed by mountains and the sea,
and the Acropolis and the Parthenon
above us seen from different sides all day,
from here and from places in the city,
the Plaka and Anafiotika
or further north, where winding streets connect
Monastiraki Square with the Agora
and the temple of Hephaestus in the part
of the city where the smiths and artisans
used to live who were his mortal counterparts.
Wherever we went we started and ended
among the scarlet poppies, the wild oats,
the olive trees and the tall cypresses,
each of us alone with her or his thoughts,

but for the time a polity of six,
half a Pantheon, three generations.
All around us were the other people,
mostly in couples or family parties,
some in groups of friends, some single spirits
tasting solitude in a perfect setting.
Hill of the Muses, Philopappos Hill,
we shall not miss you, we shall take you with us.

10: Fly Away Home

I swear as soon as we crossed the channel
the clouds began to look Constabelian –
piled up in cairns sculpted with light and shade
to show their mass and shape, airy but solid.
Before that the woman with the window seat
said France had been utterly without sun.
Perhaps the clouds there were by Edouard Manet,
master of melancholia, or Monet,
master of metamorphosis. Switzerland
and everything from the moment we climbed
out of the plain of Athens airport, ringed
by barren mountains, seemed to be cloudless,
though some of the Adriatic's eastern coast
looked a bit hazy when I craned to see.
The shores below made me want to jump out,
bays and headlands bounded by a bold curve
of continuous yellow like a ribbon
with the retaining thread it was packed in snipped
and dropped with the folds freely loosening.
It took a moment to believe all that
brightness must be miles of sandy beaches,
from that height looking utterly unspoiled
and deserted, waiting for us to swim there.

The white peaks and ridges of the mountains
round St Moritz seemed to stretch for ever
and be very high and under the white fur
to be bleak and desolate but here and there
I saw what looked no more than villages,
wondering what access to them was like
in winter, and some fertile postage stamps.

As we circled waiting permission to land
we had clear views of the Shard and the Dome,
Canary Wharf and all of central London,
and many housing estates which from the air
look, as even mountains can after a while,
quite like each other, and I couldn't help
feeling we had been in a wealthy country
and were shrinking home to a poor one, although
in terms of economics at the moment
as some know too well, the reverse is true.

We came out at last from Terminal 5
at six in the evening BST, to face
a fierce cold easterly and blinding glare
from the westering sun. When we'd found the car,
and you were sitting inside already,
I called you out to see, close by, a skylark
dipping and rising, singing his skylark song
against a daylight moon more than half full,
and as we gazed and listened the bird rose,
still singing, and became a dot and then,
though we were watching very carefully,
suddenly was nowhere to be seen, though still
the clear, enchanting music fell on us.